Termite

**Karen Hartley,
Chris Macro
and Philip Taylor**

Heinemann
LIBRARY

First published in Great Britain by Heinemann Library
Halley Court, Jordan Hill, Oxford OX2 8EJ
a division of Reed Educational and Professional Publishing Ltd.
Heinemann is a registered trademark of Reed Educational & Professional Publishing Limited.

OXFORD MELBOURNE AUCKLAND
JOHANNESBURG BLANTYRE GABORONE
IBADAN PORTSMOUTH NH CHICAGO

Designed by Celia Floyd
Illustrations by Alan Fraser [Pennant Illustration]
Printed and bound in Hong Kong/China by South China Printing Co. Ltd.

03 02 01 00 99
10 9 8 7 6 5 4 3 2 1

ISBN 0 431 01684 4

British Library Cataloguing in Publication Data

Hartley, Karen
    Termite. - (Bug books)
    1.Termite - Juvenile literature
    I.Title II.Macro, Chris
    595.7'36

Acknowledgements

The Publishers would like to thank the following for permission to reproduce photographs:
Ardea: I Beames p24, H Dossenbach pp4, 8, 10, 15, P Goetgheluck p20, J Mason p17, P Steyn p25, A Warren p19; Bruce Coleman Ltd: G Bingham pp18, 29, J Burton pp14, 23, G Cubitt pp16, 26, K Taylor pp6, 13, 28; NHPA: A Bannister p11; Okapia: A Root p22, Dr F Sauer p27; Oxford Scientific Films: M Coe p7, S Morris pp9, 12, P Murray p5, A Root p21.

Cover photograph: Gareth Boden (child); A Bannister, NHPA (termite).

Any words appearing in the text in bold, **like this**, are explained in the Glossary.

Contents

What are termites?

Termites are small **insects** with soft bodies. Termites all have different jobs to do. Some have babies, some do the work and some keep enemies away.

Some termites live in the wood of trees. Some live in the soil. Sometimes millions of termites live together in one big nest. These are called **termite mounds**.

What do termites look like?

Not all termites look the same. They all have six legs, a head and a body. The **soldiers** are blind. They have dark-coloured heads and strong legs and jaws.

Flying termites, who grow up to be **kings** and **queens**, have four wings. They have many eyes. **Worker** termites have pale bodies and they have no eyes or ears.

How big are termites?

When the **queen** is laying eggs her body swells up. She will probably be as long as a man's finger. The **king** is much smaller. He is about the same size as your big toe.

The **workers** are the smallest termites. They are about the size of your fingernail. The **soldiers** are a little bigger.

How are termites born?

The **king** and **queen** live in a special room in the termite nest. The queen lays hundreds of eggs in an hour. At first the eggs only **hatch** into **workers**.

The older workers look after the eggs which hatch into baby termites called **nymphs**. As they grow they become workers, **soldiers** or flying termites.

How do termites grow?

As the **nymph** gets older its body grows longer and the flying termites begin to be able to see. Their bodies turn black and their wings grow.

As the **soldiers** grow, their heads get very big and they grow sharp claws. When the termites grow too big for their skin, a new skin is made and the old one drops off.

What do termites eat?

Some termites eat wood and if they get into houses they also eat paper and cloth. **Workers** chew the food and put it into the mouths of the other termites.

Some termites eat plants. They like grass, leaves and dry soil. Some termites eat a sort of **fungus** which they make inside their nest.

Which animals attack termites?

Ants attack termites. The **soldier** termites fight the enemies. This **termite mound** is being attacked by flying ants.

Birds and other animals also attack termites. This termite has been caught in a spider's web. Sometimes people try to kill termites because they do so much damage to houses.

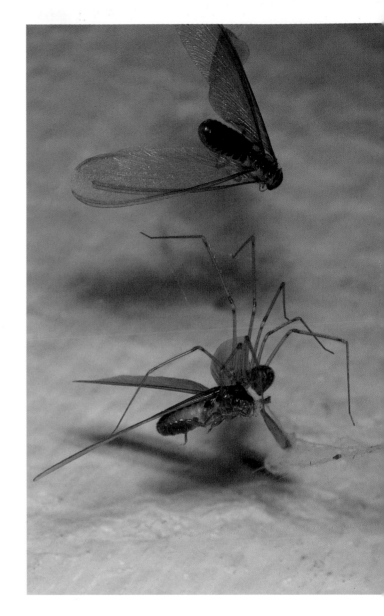

Where do termites live?

Most termites live in Africa, Australia and parts of America. Some live in very big mounds which they make with bits of soil mixed with **saliva**.

Some termites make nests in trees. They make the nests from something that looks like cardboard. They make it from chewed up wood and **body waste**.

How do termites move?

Workers and **soldiers** often walk in lines carrying leaves and seeds back to the nest. They scurry along very quickly on their six legs.

When it is time for the flying termites to leave the nest, they all fly away together. Most of them die but some find a place to start a new nest.

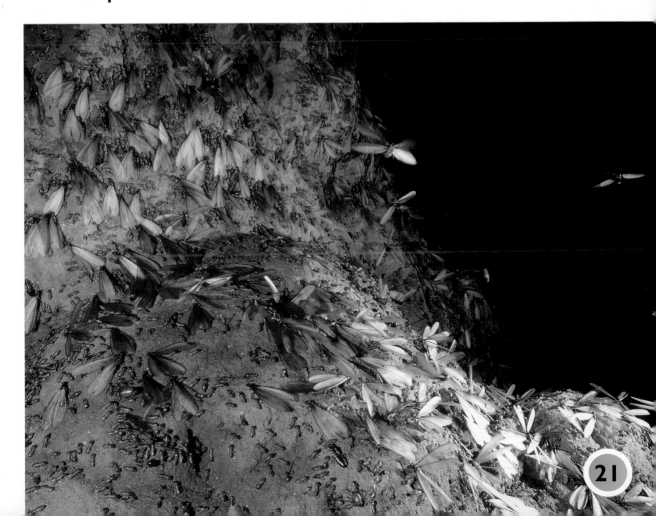

How long do termites live?

The **king** and the **queen** stay in the nest where they are safe. They may live for about thirty years. The **workers** and **soldiers** may only live for a few months.

Most of the flying termites do not live for very long. When they leave the nest they cannot fly very high and many are eaten by birds and other animals.

What do termites do?

The **worker** termites are very clever. They make the nest and build tunnels inside so that it will keep cool. They also feed the young.

The **king** and **queen** stay in their special room. When the queen is laying eggs she is so big that she cannot move. It is the **soldiers**' job to guard the entrance to the nest.

How are termites special?

Worker termites are deaf and blind but they can find their way back to the nest. When they go out they leave a trail and they smell this trail when they are coming home.

Termites can tell when other termites are near. If they are frightened they tap their heads on the ground. They can feel the ground move when other termites tap.

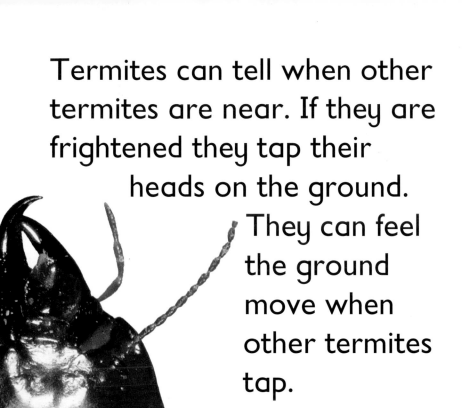

Thinking about termites

What do you think these termites eat?

How do you think they made the nest?

Which kind of termite would have built the nest?

This is a **soldier** termite.

Can you think why it has big jaws ?

What important job does the soldier do?

Bug map

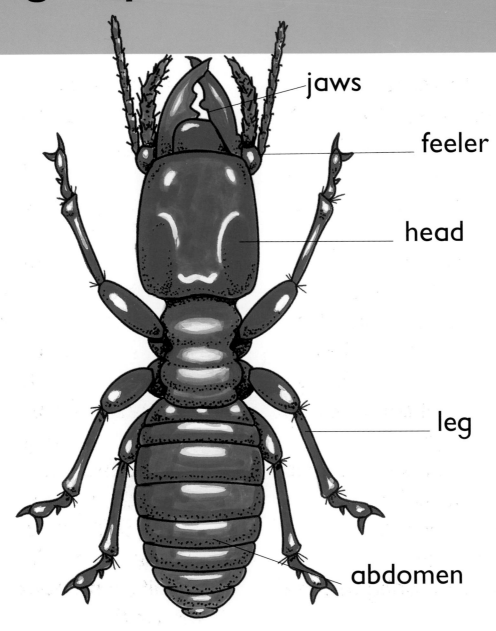

jaws

feeler

head

leg

abdomen

a soldier termite

Glossary

body waste when you go to the toilet you get rid of body waste

fungus this is a kind of mould which grows in the termites' nest. The termites make this with their bodies.

hatch when a baby animal comes out of its egg

insect a small animal with six legs

king the father termite

nymph baby termite

queen the mother termite which lays the eggs

saliva this is like the spit which is in your mouth

soldier the termite who attacks enemies and guards the nest

termite mounds very big nests which termites make above the ground. They make these with chewed up grass, bits of soil and saliva.

worker the small termite who does all the work

Index